W9-CJP-581

Published in 2013 by The Rosen Publishing Group, Inc.
29 East 21st Street, New York, NY 10010

Photo Credits: **KEY** tl=top left; tc=top center; tr=top right; cl=center left; c=center; cr=center right; bl=bottom left; bc=bottom center; br=bottom right

CBT = Corbis; DT = Dreamstime; GI = Getty Images; iS = istockphoto.com; SH = Shutterstock; TPL = photolibrary.com

6bc TPL; **9**tl SH; **13**tc iS; **14**cl TPL; **15**cr, tl TPL; **16**tr iS; **17**tc, tr GI; **18**c DT; bc GI; **20**bc iS; cr, cr TPL; **21**br TPL; **22**bl iS; **24**tl, tr GI; **25**c CBT; **27**bc, tc CBT; **28**bl, cr, tl SH; **29**br, cl iS; tr SH
All illustrations copyright Weldon Owen Pty Ltd

Weldon Owen Pty Ltd
Managing Director: Kay Scarlett
Creative Director: Sue Burk
Publisher: Helen Bateman
Senior Vice President, International Sales: Stuart Laurence
Vice President Sales North America: Ellen Towell
Administration Manager, International Sales: Kristine Ravn

Library of Congress Cataloging-in-Publication Data

Coupe, Robert.
Vanishing ice / by Robert Coupe. — 1st ed.
    p. cm. — (Discovery education: the environment)
Includes index.
ISBN 978-1-4488-7892-5 (library binding) — ISBN 978-1-4488-7980-9 (pbk.) —
ISBN 978-1-4488-7986-1 (6-pack)
1. Ice sheets—Juvenile literature. 2. Ice caps—Juvenile literature. 3. Climatic changes—Juvenile literature. 4. Global warming—Juvenile literature. I. Title.
GB2403.8.C68 2013
551.31—dc23
                    2011050674

Manufactured in the United States of America

CPSIA Compliance Information: Batch #SW12PK: For Further Information contact Rosen Publishing, New York, New York at 1-800-237-9932

Discovery
EDUCATION™

THE ENVIRONMENT

VANISHING ICE

ROBERT COUPE

PowerKiDS
press.

New York

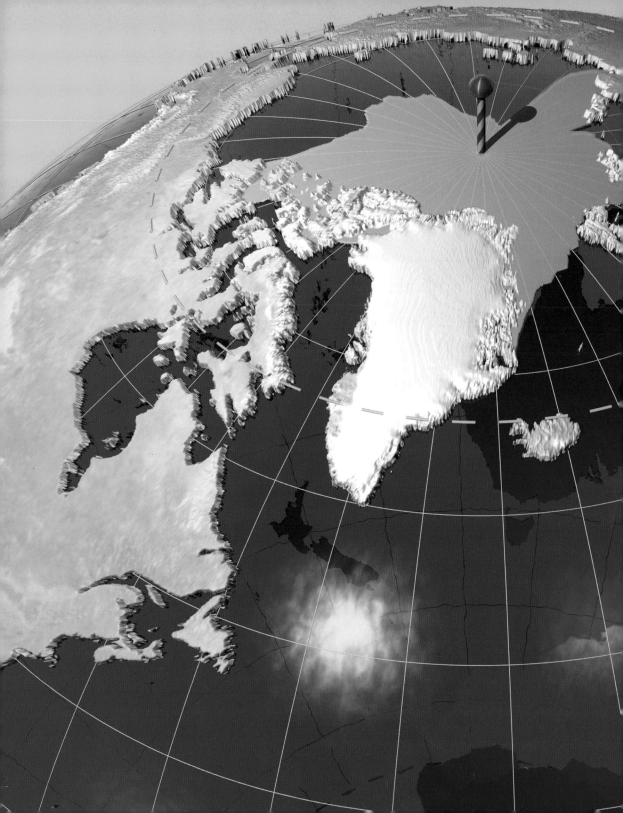

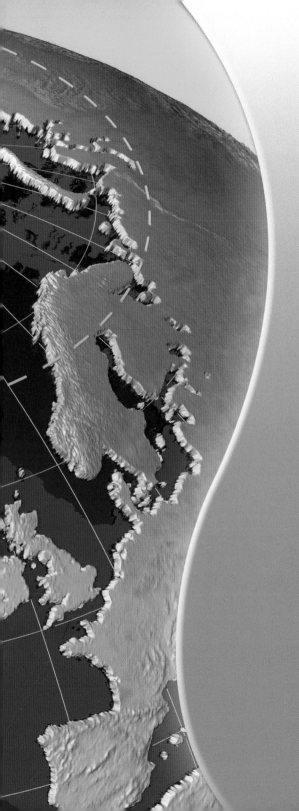

Contents

Polar Worlds

There is no colder place on Earth than the polar regions—those areas around the North and South poles. The northern polar region is called the Arctic; the southern region is the Antarctic. It is so cold because in polar regions, the Sun's rays hit the ground at a very low angle, not directly from above. So the rays provide less heat than they do in other parts of the world.

The freezing polar landscapes are covered in ice. Snow that falls there never melts entirely. Instead, it accumulates and gradually forms glaciers and very thick ice sheets. Seas around the poles also freeze over, some of them all year-round.

That's Amazing!

The lowest temperature recorded anywhere on Earth was in Antarctica. It was a freezing −128.6°F (−89.2°C). On many winter days at the poles, the Sun does not rise at all.

Arctic ice sheet
The Greenland ice sheet is a huge glacier that covers most of Greenland.

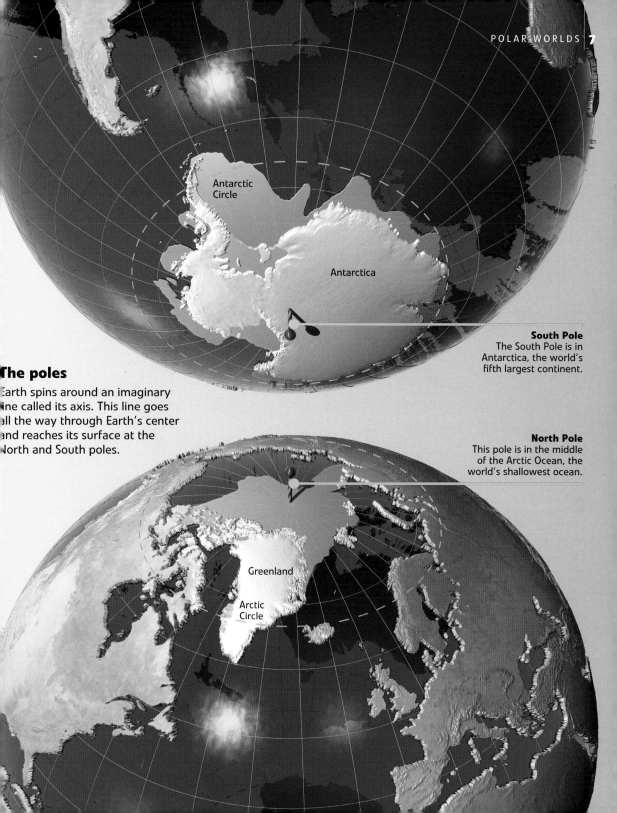

Antarctic
Circle

Antarctica

South Pole
The South Pole is in
Antarctica, the world's
fifth largest continent.

The poles

Earth spins around an imaginary
line called its axis. This line goes
all the way through Earth's center
and reaches its surface at the
North and South poles.

North Pole
This pole is in the middle
of the Arctic Ocean, the
world's shallowest ocean.

Greenland

Arctic
Circle

Icy Environments

The vast ice sheets in polar regions can cover areas as big as 20,000 square miles (52,000 km²) or more. Ice sheets over land are called continental sheets. There are now only three continental sheets left. Two of them are in Antarctica, and they are separated by a range of mountains. The other ice sheet is in the Arctic and covers 85 percent of Greenland. The ice around the North Pole is frozen sea ice.

The weight of the ice at the center of a continental ice sheet forces ice to spread outward. The ice spreads from the edge of the land out into the surrounding sea, where it forms an ice shelf. Parts of ice shelves break away to form icebergs.

That's Amazing!

The Greenland ice sheet has an average thickness of 5,000 feet (1.5 km), but the Antarctic ice sheets are, in some places, more than 2.8 miles (4.5 km) thick.

Pack ice
Ice can freeze along the coast or drift on the surface and be forced into pack ice.

Sea ice
Sea ice is made from frozen seawater, whereas icebergs are compacted snow, so are made of fresh water.

Iceberg
Less than a quarter of an iceberg is above the water. Most of it is underwater and difficult to see.

Icebergs

The largest known icebergs have broken away from the ice shelves of Antarctica. Some of them are hundreds of miles (km) long. Most icebergs in the north are from the edge of the Greenland ice sheet.

Ice shelf
Right at the edge of a continental ice sheet, there is an area of floating ice, which is called an ice shelf.

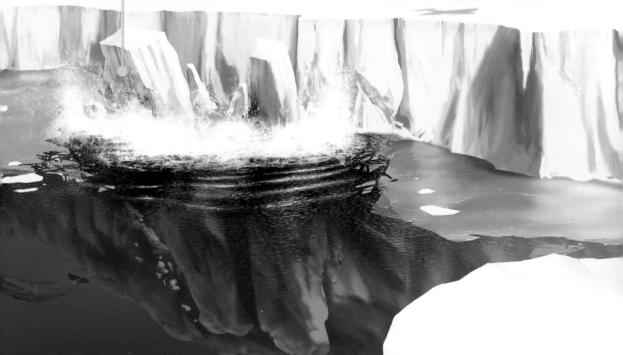

Calving
Icebergs break away from the ice shelf at the edge of an ice sheet or from a glacier. This is called calving.

Tracking
Aircraft use radar to keep track of icebergs. Ships on regular patrols look out for and warn about them.

Life On Ice

Earth's polar regions are home to many land and marine animals. In the Arctic, polar bears, wolves, gulls, snowy owls, Arctic foxes, beluga whales, and walruses are among the species that have adapted to the harsh conditions there. Many of the world's penguin species live on or near Antarctica, and seals, whales, krill, and a range of fish species abound in the Antarctic waters of the Southern Ocean.

Traditional human dwellers of the Arctic, such as the Inuit, have lived in the cold north for thousands of years. They have developed hunting techniques, building methods, and protective clothing that allow them to live, work, and survive in the freezing conditions.

Narwhal
This whale swims in Arctic waters and feeds on fish, squid, and shrimp. Only male narwhals grow the long tusk, which is an extension of one of their teeth.

IGLOO

The igloo is the traditional Inuit dwelling. It is built of blocks of hard, compacted snow, which are placed in a spiral pattern until they form a dome. A tunnel leads from the outside into the igloo. Most Inuit now live in wooden houses in villages, but they still build and live in igloos during winter hunting trips.

Emperor penguin

King penguin

Chinstrap penguin

Adélie penguin

Penguins
Four of the 17 different species of penguin live in the Antarctic polar region. These penguins have fat under their skin and thick feathers to protect them from the cold. Others, such as the King penguin, live in the subantarctic region.

Dressed for the cold
The Inuit use animal skins for clothing that keeps out the cold. Winter clothes are made of caribou, or reindeer, fur. One layer faces inward, the other faces outward. In spring and summer, lighter sealskins are warm enough.

Ice and Glaciers

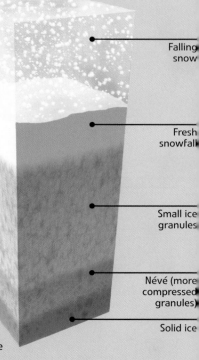

A glacier forms when snow that falls on the ground does not melt but builds up, year after year. The lower layers of the snow eventually turn into ice. The force of gravity gradually pulls this mass of ice and snow downhill toward the sea. In some places, it moves over flat land in a wide ice sheet. In other places, it moves through valleys between high mountains. It can even wear away parts of the land and form valleys.

Sometimes, glacial ice that gets trapped in an enclosed mountain area can melt and form lakes. Water from these meltwater lakes can then flow down through narrow channels to the sea. Glaciers cover about one tenth of Earth's total land surface.

Falling snow

Fresh snowfall

Small ice granules

Névé (more compressed granules)

Solid ice

From snow to ice
Snow underneath a fresh snowfall forms ice granules. The weight of more snow squeezes air out of the granules and forms névé, then solid ice.

Different glaciers
Glaciers form and flow in different ways. Cirque glaciers, for example, form in hollow mountain valleys. Ice from them eventually flows through narrow openings to form wider valley glaciers.

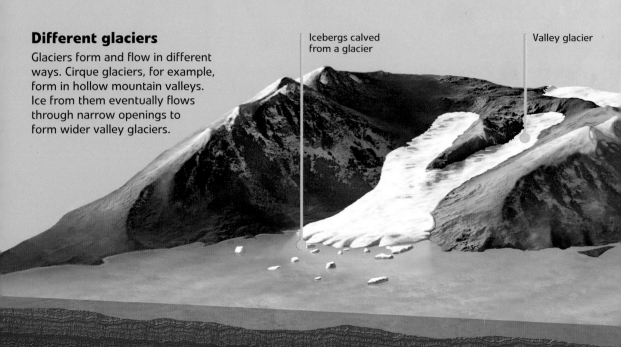

Icebergs calved from a glacier

Valley glacier

Perito Moreno Glacier
The end of the Perito Moreno Glacier, in Argentina, stretches for 3 miles (5 km) across the surface of Lake Argentino.

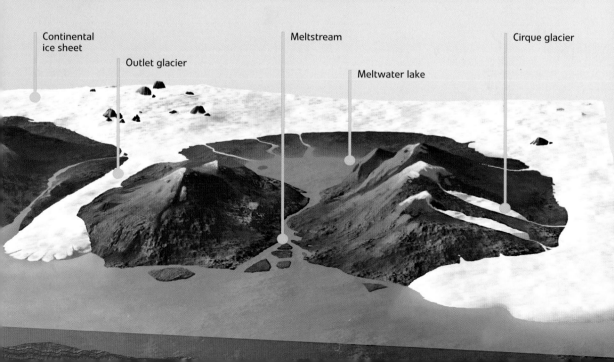

Continental
ice sheet

Outlet glacier

Meltstream

Meltwater lake

Cirque glacier

Evidence of Melting Ice

Most scientists who study Earth's climate now agree that it is becoming steadily warmer and that human beings are at least partly responsible for this. In many parts of the world, summers are becoming hotter and winters warmer. Average temperatures are on the rise. This trend is called global warming.

One obvious effect of global warming is that some of the vast ice sheets that cover much of the polar regions are becoming smaller every year. Another effect of global warming is that glaciers, which have slowly moved down through mountain valleys for centuries, are now melting. Some are disappearing slowly; others are getting smaller at a very fast rate.

Swiss glacier in 2002
Trift Glacier in Switzerland began to melt and form a lake in 2001. This photo shows what it looks like one year later.

January 31, 2002   February 17, 2002

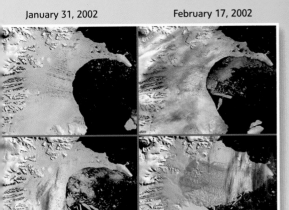

February 23, 2002   March 5, 2002

Larsen Ice Shelf, Antarctica

These satellite images of the Larsen Ice Shelf were taken between January 31 and March 5, 2002. They show how, in just over a month, a huge section of the ice shelf broke away to form the masses of small icebergs that can be seen in the picture on the bottom right.

Disappearing glaciers

The map below shows the location of the world's glaciers and the rate at which they are retreating.

KEY

☐ Polar glaciers: almost all in retreat
● Glaciers: almost all in retreat
● Glaciers: more than half in retreat
● Glaciers: some in retreat

Swiss glacier in 2003
Another year later, the lake had grown much bigger. The glacier had retreated farther up the valley.

Why Is the Ice Melting?

During Earth's long history, the world has warmed and cooled many times. But it is only in recent times that humans have had a real influence on the planet's climate.

The world is heating up now mainly because factories, power plants, and forms of transportation are burning large amounts of coal, oil, and gas. When these fossil fuels burn, they release into the atmosphere huge quantities of carbon dioxide and other greenhouse gases. Greenhouse gases trap heat inside the atmosphere and cause it to get hotter.

Into the atmosphere
The eight towers of this coal-fired electricity power station in Leicestershire, UK, are pumping huge amounts of greenhouse gases into the atmosphere.

The greenhouse effect
Earth's surface soaks up the Sun's energy and releases it as heat. Carbon dioxide and other gases absorb this. If there is too much carbon dioxide, more heat stays in the atmosphere.

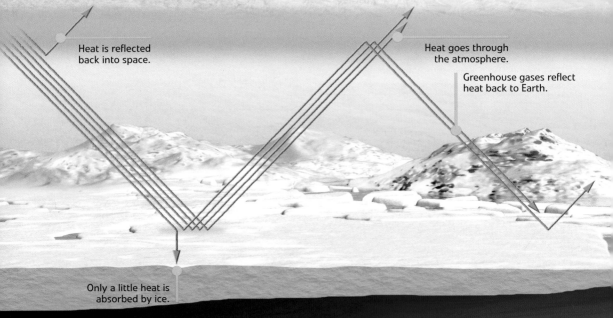

Heat is reflected back into space.

Heat goes through the atmosphere.

Greenhouse gases reflect heat back to Earth.

Only a little heat is absorbed by ice.

Reflecting energy
In polar regions, ice reflects most of the Sun's warming energy back up into the atmosphere.

Sending it back
Some of this warmth is trapped by greenhouse gases in the atmosphere and reflected back.

MELTING FASTER

When the Sun's rays fall on the white blanket of ice and snow that covers large parts of the polar regions, most of the warmth is reflected from the shiny white surface back into the atmosphere. But as more of the ice covering melts, more of the Sun's rays strike the land or the sea. Most of the warmth is absorbed by those surfaces; very little is reflected. As the sea and land warm up, the ice covering melts even faster.

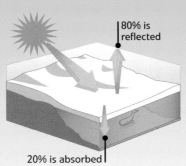

80% is reflected

20% is absorbed

Greater reflection
Most of the warmth from the Sun's rays bounces back up from the shiny white surface of the ice in the world's polar regions.

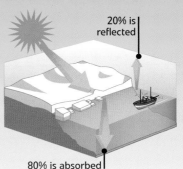

20% is reflected

80% is absorbed

Greater absorption
As more ice melts, much more of the Sun's rays and warmth are absorbed by the land and water. This leads to more and faster melting.

Heat is reflected back into space.

Heat goes through the atmosphere.

More heat is retained.

Heat absorbed by land and open water radiates upward.

Absorbing energy
Land and oceans do not reflect much energy. They absorb it and heat the ocean, land, and air.

A warming cycle
As the air warms up, more ice melts. The land and sea then absorb more of the Sun's warmth.

Effects in Antarctica

An ice shelf collapses
This huge Antarctic ice shelf broke up in 2002. It sent icebergs into the sea and made large crevasses in the glacier that flowed into it.

Until quite recently, it was not clear that the Antarctic polar region was becoming warmer. But recent research has showed that it is in fact warming up at about the same rate as most of the rest of the planet. We now know that temperatures there have increased by 5.4°F (3°C) over the last 50 years. The Arctic, in contrast, is warming about twice as fast.

Warming in the Antarctic has resulted in the dramatic collapse of a number of ice shelves around the continent's coast. As these vast masses of ice fall away into the sea, the seas around Antarctica become warmer. This results in yet more ice around the coastline starting to melt.

VOLCANIC ASH

Mount Belinda is a volcano in Antarctica. Between 2001 and 2007, it erupted several times, and dark ash settled on nearby icebergs and glaciers. These darkened surfaces absorbed more heat from the Sun, which resulted in more snow and ice melting.

Mount Belinda

Feeding on krill

Krill are tiny marine creatures that live in all the world's oceans. They thrive in the cold Antarctic waters. Whales, squid, penguins, and seals are Antarctic animals that feed mainly on krill. As the waters of the Antarctic get warmer, there are fewer krill to be found there. This is a problem for the animals right along the food chain that depend on krill for their survival.

Gray-headed albatross
This bird nests in or near the Antarctic. Squid is its main food, and squid mostly eat krill. So krill is important to its survival.

Macaroni penguin
Krill is this penguin's main food. As the krill declines, it is harder for the penguins to find the food they need.

Sperm whales
Sperm whales live in all the world's oceans and they feed mostly on krill-eating squid. Ultimately, they depend on the krill in the Antarctic.

Effects in the Arctic

Temperatures in the Arctic polar region are rising almost twice as fast as temperatures in many other parts of the world. Arctic sea ice is disappearing at an alarming rate. Not only is the ice retreating, throughout the Arctic it is also much thinner than it used to be. Scientists claim that a further rise in the average world temperature of only 2.7°F (1.5°C) could cause the Greenland ice sheet, the second largest ice sheet on Earth, to shrink dramatically.

As the ice melts, the seas become warmer, and the ocean currents start to flow differently. These changes are already having an effect on the climate of this region and on the people and animals that live there.

Coastal settlements
Inuit villages could be threatened as sea levels rise and the coast is eroded because of global warming.

ICE RETREAT

These satellite photos of ice in the Arctic polar region reveal just how quickly the ice cover is shrinking there. In just under 30 years, more than one third of Arctic ice has disappeared. This includes both the sea ice and the ice sheet of the northern polar region.

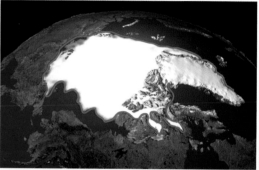
1979

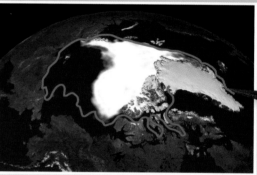
2007

The blue whale

Blue whales are the largest animals on Earth. They spend summer in polar seas and migrate to warmer oceans in winter. During the twentieth century, they were hunted almost to extinction. Hunting them was banned in 1967. Blue whales feed on tiny krill, but as the oceans have become warmer, krill numbers have declined. This is another threat to these giants of the sea.

Blue whale

NORTH AMERICA
EUROPE
ASIA
AFRICA
SOUTH AMERICA
AUSTRALIA
ANTARCTIC

KEY
Winter migration

Endangered
Ribbon seals rely on the Arctic sea ice for survival. Melting ice is causing loss of habitat, and their numbers have decreased.

Fin whale
Fin whales feed mainly on krill. Numbers are declining, and they may even become extinct.

Polar Bears and Ice

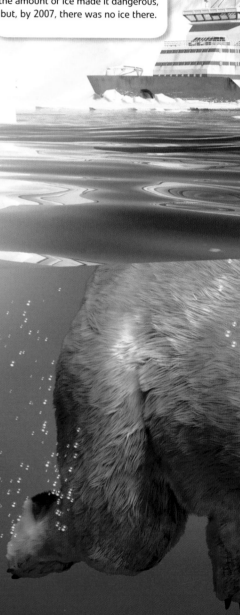

Polar bears are huge and powerful animals that live on and around the sea ice in the Arctic. They are fierce and skillful hunters that eat mainly seals, although they also catch caribou, fish, and some whales. When they hunt, they often wait beside holes in the ice for seals to poke their snout up out of the water to breathe. Then the bears grab them. Polar bears also chase seals and other animals across the surface of the ice.

Global warming is a big threat to polar bears. As the seas warm up, there is less sea ice on which they can hunt. Sometimes, ice platforms are spread too far apart for the bears to swim between. In some parts of the Arctic, the number of polar bears has already started to fall.

Did You Know?

The Northwest Passage is a sea route between the Atlantic and Pacific oceans, north of Canada. For centuries, the amount of ice made it dangerous, but, by 2007, there was no ice there.

Stranded
A polar bear is stranded on a small ice floe, too far from the solid sea ice on which it hunts.

A longer swim

In many parts of the Arctic, as the sea ice melts and areas of open water get larger, polar bears have to swim much farther to find ice platforms on which they can hunt.

Shishmaref
Rising sea levels mean higher tides. Higher tides erode coastlines and destroy coastal homes, like this one in the Inuit town of Shishmaref, on the coast of Alaska.

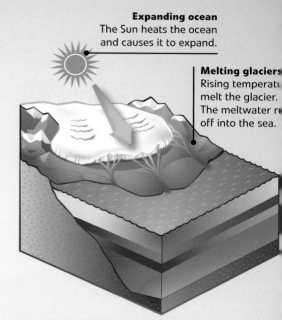

Expanding ocean
The Sun heats the ocean and causes it to expand.

Melting glaciers
Rising temperatu melt the glacier. The meltwater r off into the sea.

Why are sea levels rising?
Melting glaciers and oceans that expand as they warm up account for about half the rise in sea levels. Scientists are not sure what other factors are causing sea levels to rise.

Warming and Rising Seas

As temperatures increase and polar ice continues to melt, sea levels around the world will rise. In the last 100 years, seas have already risen by 8 inches (20 cm). But most climatologists now agree that rises in the future will occur at a much faster rate.

The ice sheets and glaciers in polar regions hold vast amounts of water. The Antarctic ice sheet alone holds 70 percent of the world's freshwater. If it melted completely, sea levels would rise by 230 feet (70 m). This is unlikely to happen. Even if it did, it would take thousands of years. But many climatologists believe that by 2100, rising sea levels will affect billions of people, especially those in poorer countries.

HOW FAR WILL SEA LEVELS RISE?

If sea levels keep rising at the current rate, they will be about 19 inches (48 cm) higher by the year 2100. However, if increased warming results in more ice melting in Greenland or Antarctica, this could push up sea levels by 39 inches (100 cm) or more.

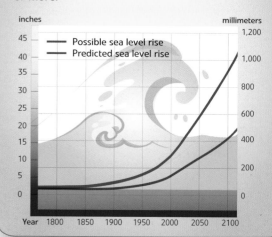

inches

	millimeters

— Possible sea level rise
— Predicted sea level rise

Year 1800 1850 1900 1950 2000 2050 2100

●nice

●als carry water from the sea ●ht through the city of Venice, ●ly. The canals have always ●oded. But now, as sea levels ●e, the floodwaters are higher, ●d flooding is more frequent.

Scientists at Work

S cientists have developed ways to search beneath the Arctic and Antarctic ice. Radar, carried by space satellites and airplanes, can pick up reflections from surfaces deep beneath the ice.

Ice cores—cylinders of ice drilled from ice sheets and glaciers—provide evidence of how the climate has changed over thousands of years, as well as clues about how it might change in the future. Studies on ice cores, and the air trapped inside them, have shown that, in the past, temperatures were higher when there were high levels of carbon dioxide in the air. Ice cores can be more than 1 mile (1.6 km) long. The longer they are, the more they tell us about the distant past.

Retreating ice
This graph shows how much ice is expected to melt in the north and south polar regions in the twenty-first century. The north could lose more than 40 percent of its ice.

Ice core
A scientist holds a small section of an ice core that was drilled from deep in the ice in Antarctica.

Weather balloon
This balloon carries instruments into the atmosphere. When it returns, the instruments bring back information about weather, air pressure, and gases present at different levels.

ar bear study
researcher in Manitoba,
ada, holds a polar bear cub.
s part of a team studying
polar bears are reacting to
nges in their environment.

Fact File

Rising sea levels

It is just possible that by 2100 sea levels will rise by 39 inches (100 cm). Even just half that rise will cause flooding in many coastal and low-lying parts of the world.

Drier conditions

Hotter, drier climates are drying out lands in many parts of the world. It is getting more difficult to cultivate crops in those areas and feed large human populations.

Melting ice sheets

The ice sheet and sea ice in the Arctic are melting so quickly that by 2050 there could be no ice cover there in the summer months. Scientists used to think this would not happen until 2100.

Shrinking glaciers

Glaciers of the northern Andes mountains in South America have been getting smaller for decades. But they began to retreat more quickly during the 1990s.

Thinning glaciers

The glaciers in the Himalayas, in northern Asia, have been steadily retreating and getting thinner over the last half-century. This has been accelerating in the last decade.

Expanding glaciers

Some New Zealand glaciers have grown in the last two decades because of increased rainfall. But glaciers in other regions of the Pacific have retreated.

Glossary

adapted (uh-DAP-ted)
Changed in ways to live and survive in a particular place.

air pressure (EHR PREH-shur)
The force created by the weight of the air in the atmosphere.

Antarctic Circle
(ant-ARK-tik SUR-kul)
An imaginary line around Earth that marks the edge of the Antarctic region.

Antarctica
(ant-AHRK-tih-kuh) The huge, ice-covered continent that surrounds the South Pole.

Arctic (ARK-tik) The cold, icy part of the world that surrounds the North Pole.

Arctic Circle
(ARK-tik SUR-kul) An imaginary line around Earth that marks the edge of the Arctic region.

atmosphere (AT-muh-sfeer)
Layers of gases that surround a planet, such as Earth. Outside Earth's atmosphere is the region known as "space."

carbon dioxide
(KAHR-bun dy-OK-syd)
A colorless gas that has no odor. It is formed when fuels and other materials are burned. Humans and other animals breathe out carbon dioxide.

climate (KLY-mut) Weather conditions, such as average rainfall and temperature, that normally occur over a long period in a particular part of the world.

climatologists
(kly-muh-TAH-luh-jist) Scientists who study climate patterns around the world.

continent (KON-tuh-nent)
One of the seven large landmasses on Earth—Africa, Antarctica, Asia, Australia, Europe, North America, and South America.

crevasse (krih-VAS) A wide, deep split in a glacier or an ice sheet.

Earth's axis (URTHS AK-sus)
An imaginary line that goes through the center of Earth from the North Pole to the South Pole. Earth is constantly spinning around its axis.

fossil fuels (FO-sul FYOOLZ)
Coal, oil, gas, and other substances that form over thousands of years inside Earth, and are used as fuel.

glacier (GLAY-shur) A huge mass of ice formed from snow that has been compressed as more and more snow falls on it. Glaciers flow slowly over land over thousands of years.

global warming
(GLOH-bul WAWRM-ing)
A steady and continuing increase in the average temperature of Earth's atmosphere.

gravity (GRA-vih-tee) The force that pulls objects down to the ground and keeps Earth and other planets moving in orbit around the Sun.

greenhouse gases
(GREEN-hows GAS-ez) Gases, such as carbon dioxide and methane, that can trap heat inside Earth's atmosphere and stop it from escaping.

Greenland (GREEN-lund) The world's largest island. Situated in the North Atlantic Ocean, four fifths of its area is covered by a huge ice sheet.

habitat (HA-buh-tat) The area or the kind of surroundings in which an animal or plant lives and grows.

Himalayas (hih-muh-LAY-uhz) A mountain range in southern Asia between India and Tibet. The highest mountain on Earth, Mount Everest, and many other very high mountains, are in the Himalayas.

iceberg (YS-burg) A large, floating block of ice that has broken away from a glacier.

ice floe (EYES FLOH) A flat, moving piece of sea ice, usually less than 6 miles (10 km) long.

ice sheet (EYES SHEET) A large mass of ice formed on top of land. It can be more than 1 mile (1.6 km) deep and can cover an area of up to 20,000 square miles (52,000 km²).

ice shelf (EYES SHELF) A large slab of ice that floats on the water, but is still attached to an ice sheet. The world's largest ice shelves are in Antarctica.

Inuit (IH-new-it) A group of people who live in the Arctic regions of Canada, Alaska, Greenland, and the northeast part of Asia.

krill (KRIL) Tiny shrimplike marine animals. Vast numbers of krill live in the world's oceans and are a key food source for fish, whales, and other marine creatures.

névé (nay-VAY) Very small pieces, or granules, of almost frozen snow that are packed closely together. Névé form one of the layers of a glacier.

North Pole (NORTH POHL) The northern end of Earth's axis. It is the point on Earth that is farthest north.

outlet glacier (OWT-let GLAY-shur) A glacier that takes ice from an ice sheet.

radar (RAY-dahr) Short for "radio detecting and ranging," radar is a way of finding the location and speed of a moving vehicle, or the shape and depth of a landform or ice sheet. It does this by measuring the time and direction of a radio wave that comes back from the object.

satellite images (SA-tih-lyt IH-mij-es) Photographs sent back to Earth from satellites in space orbiting around Earth.

South Pole (SOWTH POHL) The southern end of Earth's axis. It is the point on Earth that is farthest south.

subantarctic region (sub-ant-ARK-tik REE-jun) The part of the world that is just north of the Antarctic Circle.

Index

Websites

Due to the changing nature of Internet links, PowerKids Press has developed an online list of websites related to the subject of this book. This site is updated regularly. Please use this link to access the list: www.powerkidslinks.com/disc/ice/